A-Z of Aphrodisia

A-Z of Aphrodisia

DIANA WARBURTON

QUARTET BOOKS

London   New York

First published by Quartet Books Limited 1986
A member of the Namara Group
27–29 Goodge Street, London W1P 1FD

Copyright © by Diana Warburton 1986

British Library Cataloguing in Publication Data
Warburton, Diana
    A-Z of aphrodisia
    1. Aphrodisiacs — Dictionaries
    I. Title
    615'.766   HQ12

    ISBN 0–7043–2599–3

Design by Namara
Typeset by M.C. Typeset Limited, Chatham, Kent
Printed and bound by Nene Litho and Woolnough Bookbinding
both of Irthlingborough, Northants.

Through the Jade Gate we enter this life
Once born we are forever seeking to return.
How many men wake in the night
Their Iron Rod stiff with desire;
And with this eternal truth that other message —
That the joy of life and everlasting youth
Is found in the same place as his creation.

Lewd Tales from China (1927)
YONEDA YUTARO

Acknowledgement

I am most grateful
to my son,
Felix,
for his witty scholarship.

In loving memory
Roger and Minora Money Kyrle

Contents

Foreword

THE ANCIENT FERTILITY goddess to whom men prayed for a good harvest, healthy cattle and children to perpetuate themselves was depicted in a generous mould. As civilization advanced she slimmed down to Aphrodite/Venus, goddess of Beauty and Love from whom the word aphrodisiac was derived, defined by the dictionary as that which produces venereal desire. Lovemaking, the means of assuring fertility, had become an Art . . . Thus any food or substance symbolic of fertility (the nut, the seed or ear of corn) or which nourishes the body and improves its sexual function, or which arouses desire and enhances the quality of the act of love is fairly named an aphrodisiac. This book presents both the aphrodisiacs of legend and tradition and those which have a more practical or scientific basis. It includes such things as massage, fasting and magic rituals as well as recipes for lovers, ointments and perfumes. All of which have their place within the aphrodisia.

The History
of Aphrodisiacs
– a Quick One

LOVE IS NOT only a physical hunger but an emotional
need and the greatest of all human preoccupations.
Throughout the centuries and in all parts of the world
men have sought the means to improve the quality of
both sex and romance. The Greeks, who had a
particularly joyful approach to living and loving,
regarded life as best spent in the pursuit of pleasure.
Indulgence in sensuality was almost a religious
obligation, as it was owing to the gods to show
appreciation for the gift of the beauties of the flesh,
and indeed their gods were not slow to show them
examples. Aphrodite, goddess of Love, was also
worshipped as Aphrodite Porne (Aphrodite the whore)
and was not at all averse to the joys of illicit love, for
where love was concerned there was no sacred and
profane. The Greek attitude to love was devoid of
illusion and prudery and the Greek gods were
expressions of all that the Greeks admired and would
like to be themselves.

However, in their daily lives they aimed to live
with grace and self-control and so they used the
orgiastic festivals of the Aphrodisia and Dionysia as
safety valves to let off steam, frequently paid for by

the State. There was a flourishing trade in aphrodisiac preparations and charms, the most popular of these being obtained from the experienced Hetairae, the temple prostitutes and priestesses. The Greeks in their erotic writings favoured the use of onions, carrots, truffles, eggs, honey and pineapple as well as sturgeon (the mother of caviar), crabs and snails, shrimps and other shellfish, for fish has always been credited with being aphrodisiac by reason of its association with the sea (from whence came Venus) and its high nutritional value. The ancient Egyptians forbade their priests the eating of fish as it distracted them from their duties.

Like many others the Greeks were impressed by foreign and exotic foods and set great store by recipes from Egypt and the East. Unlike the Greek, Roman society was ruled by its passions and the Roman writer Ovid saw fit in his *Remedia Amoris* to warn them against the use of 'philtres which disturb the balance of the mind and illumine the fires of furious madness'. Caligula was said to have been turned from a reasonable Roman to a degenerate beast by the poisonous potions administered by his wife to sustain his love. Ovid advised the use of wholesome herbs and plants, and suggested that many of those aphrodisiacs in frequent use were more likely to poison than advance love's cause. 'Eat the white shallots sent from Megara, or garden herbs that aphrodisiacs are, or eggs, or honey on hymettus flowing, or nuts upon the sharp leaved pine tree growing. Erato why turn'st thou to magic art! A far more subtle way I would impart.'

The Romans added to the Greek list the genitals of various animals: the ass, the wolf and the deer, all wild or amorous by repute and thus adding sympathetic magic to the aphrodisiac feast. Horace when enquiring about a certain seaside resort asked if there were game, fish and sea urchins enough 'To warm my veins and pass into my mind, enrich me with new hopes, choice words supply, and make me comely in a lady's eye'.

Here we also find the nutritious oyster whose flesh has launched a thousand love affairs; beans, ever regarded as lust-provoking, being symbolic of fertility and used the world over in love magic; rocket grown around the phallic statues rising everywhere to Priapus son of Venus, the Roman Aphrodite, and Bacchus, god of Wine; pepper ground with nettle seed, savory and mushrooms. Amulets made of crocodiles' teeth or the skin of cranes were thought particularly effective aphrodisiacs when worn.

The Romans, alas, drew on another powerful sexual stimulant, cruelty. They delighted in the gross spectacle of the circus with its scenes of torture, degradation and death . . . 'strike so that he feels that he is dying,' said Caligula. Surrounding the Circus Maximus in Rome were many brothels to serve the appetites of men returning from the games raised to a frenzy of excitement by the spectacle. Here perhaps is a clue to why some believe that red meat is invigorating, that it brings out the beast in man. (Towards the end of the eighteenth century the

Marquis de Sade in his erotic work *Juliette* recommends meat as a sexually stimulating food, one of the characters going so far as to praise the virtues of consuming human flesh!) However, our human alimentary canal is better suited to digesting vegetable matter and too much meat is therefore best avoided when pursuing love.

It is in Roman society that we first find the idea of sexual guilt. The circus, the religious festivals such as the bacchanalia where priests and participants indulged in gross unbridled lust, and the unjust social system built on slavery perverted their morality and corrupted their attitudes to pleasure. The more decadent, repressive or chauvinist the society becomes, the more extreme will be the measures taken to combat its problems in every sphere. The Romans, surfeited with indulgences of the flesh, would have been better reverting to Ovid's simple recommendations to restore their flagging sexual energies than to rely upon orgiastic banquets with such rich and sumptuous dishes as livers of pike, peacock brains and flamingo tongues. Such luxury was intended to increase the libido and further spectacles of grossness were staged to inflame the appetites of the privileged. Erotic theatrical performances were often presented at banquets with dancing girls like those described by Juvenal: 'Perhaps you will expect the itching dances of Gades [Cadiz] while a band croons, and the girls sink to the ground and quiver to applause . . . a stimulus for languid lovers, nettles to whip rich men to life.' Some aphrodisiacs used by the Romans were frankly poisonous and ill-gotten. The Emperor Vespasian decreed that whoever had supplied an aphrodisiac potion should be fined and exiled or executed if it proved fatal. Even this did nothing to stop the traffic in such drugs. The Christian Church, fighting for survival amid all this worldly excess, fostered the notion that sexual and even sensual pleasures were wrong and unfortunately maintained this stance throughout the centuries – a far cry from the simple hedonism of the Greeks.

Since knowledge of aphrodisiacs was frequently equated with love magic (usually with good reason) it was regarded balefully by the Church, which by the Middle Ages had advanced to great influence in the major part of the Western world. The medieval lover, stricken by unrequited or impotent love, was therefore forced to seek help from irregular sources, well versed in skulduggery. Their use now shrouded with guilt, the constituents of the aphrodisiac took on a sinister tone; if sexual pleasure was to be deemed wrong, then in for a penny in for a pound! Heart of a toad, fat from the gallows victim stewed in the skull of a man – such things as these were used to influence the path of love. Thus the sensual god Pan had become the Devil, horns and tail and all, and the lovely Aphrodite/Venus was portrayed as a wicked witch waiting to ensnare the weak and sinful. What a contrast to the generous love of the Mother of Creation! However, all was not in darkness, for the more charming potions and cures known to the wise of ancient times were still remembered, their reputation reinforced by centuries of use . . . time and distance always adding to people's confidence in these matters. The mistresses of Merrie England made preparations in their kitchens laced with a loving herb or two, as had the famed witches of Thessaly in Greece (who by the way were not averse to the inclusion of the occasional foul ingredient). In Tudor England, the sumptuous feasts of roasted hogs, does, lambs, chicken, salmon and lampreys, were served with piquant sauces made by French and Italian cooks (treasured even then) who knew well the supposed properties of such cuisine: 'Woe to the cook whose sauces had no sting!' Again the diners 'intersperse the varied and exquisite repast with music and jesters and when the meal is over they fall to dancing and the embraces of the ladies'.

Herbalists and physicians were often over-hasty in attributing wondrous properties to the new foods shipped in from foreign lands. Tomatoes, known as love apples, and potatoes from Peru were said to be endowed with stimulating powers by dint of their exotic source and the great expense with which they were obtained, rarity and luxury ever being powerful aphrodisiacs, transporting the fortunate into an atmosphere far removed from the mundane. Shakespeare's Falstaff, when he wished to court the merrie wives of Windsor, cried: 'Let the sky rain potatoes!' A character in John Fletcher's play *The Loyal Subject* (1618) begs: 'Will your Lordship please to taste a fine potato? 'T'will advance your withered state, Fill your honour with noble itches.'

Holinshed noted that 'the kind of meat [food] which is obtained with most difficulty and cost, is commonly taken for the most delicate and thereupon each guest will soonest desire to feed'. However, many imported products from the Americas and from the East were rightly thought and seen 'to provoke a man's veneryous actes' in one way or another. But more of these later.

After the dissolution of the monasteries, whose

masters kept kitchens equal to those of royalty, came the land enclosures and the poor of England starved. Out of this dark depression came a Puritanism which, dispensing with the glorious pageantry of the Stuart monarchy, banned the use of spices 'which excite the passions'. It is interesting to note, however, that, a century before, Diane de Poitier the mistress of Henry II who was considered to be the most beautiful woman in France had knowingly rejected the rich courtly diet in favour of fresh fruit and vegetables. Although (according to Miss Barbara Cartland) it was said that witchcraft explained Madame's youth and their passionate love.

After the Restoration the Stuarts once more gave way to sensual and culinary excesses, though frequently too much food and wine 'made feeble their endeavours'. Carps' tongues in crusty pies and pheasants drenched with ambergris would entertain the fortunate lover. But truth to tell, the English palate never recovered from the plain fare required by the Puritans and 'good roast meat' was considered right for the Englishman, none of those saucy dishes smacking of the twin Romes with all their attendant lasciviousness. In this context it can be seen that any rich, elegant, spicy or unusual food would be considered 'synnefulle' and for this read 'aphrodisiac'. So the virtues of kickshaws (*quelques choses*) were not overlooked. Those with time and fortune enough to enjoy their senses would still employ the services of French cooks who tempted them with various 'pyes, gelyes, tartes and cremes' of mushrooms, kidneys, truffles and larks, almonds and asparagus, and 'sucking pigs served in a dish, taken from a sow as soon as farrowed, a fortnight fed with dates and

Muscadine', (Philip Massinger in *The City Madam*, 1630). These happy men appalled the likes of Samuel Pepys with their resultant 'loose amours'.

The French have long had a reputation for appreciating the pleasure of both the table and the flesh – Talleyrand said that there are two things to life, that is 'to give good dinners and to keep on fair terms with women'. The madames running the pleasure houses in eighteenth-century France served *petits soupers* illustrating well the sympathetic French alliance between food and love. They vied with one another to serve up the most excellent fare to attract the custom of the fashionable rich. The Marquis de Sade in *120 Days of Sodom* describes how the gallants and their mistresses sometimes naked, supped on elaborate dishes 'composed of white flesh of fowl and of game disguised in all manners. This was followed by a course of roasts which comprised the rarest meats imaginable; then arrived a course of cold confectionery which was soon replaced by twenty-six puddings in all figures and shapes; these were cleared away and what was removed was replaced by complete garnish of sweet pastries cold and hot; finally the dessert appeared offering a prodigious variety of fruits in spite of the season, then the ices, the chocolate and the liqueurs which were consumed at the table. As for the wines, these varied with each course.' These dishes were seasoned with pepper and ginger and other exotic spices to warm the loins; the pastries and chocolates liberally dosed with cantharides (the Spanish fly) to the detriment of many. The elegant brothel had special 'salons de préparation' where all manner of aphrodisiac pills, potions and 'parfums d'Arabie' were made, along with curious mechanical devices, all to spoil (in the true sense of the word) the clients.

The Arab traders in silk and spices also brought with them new ideas from their great Arabian civilization – a civilization which produced distinguished works of science and astronomy, medicine and philosophy from which European scholarship was ultimately derived (much of which was lost in the destruction of the great Library of Alexandria during Caesar's wars [48 B.C.] and the 'Daughter' Library burnt down in A.D. 389 by the savage bigotry of the Christian Emperor Theodosius I). They also produced a wealth of poetry and literature. Thanks to the translation from the French by Sir Richard Burton, scholar and traveller, we are privy to the curious Arabian work on love known as *The Perfumed Garden for the Soul's Delectation* by Sheikh Nefzawi written 'in a spirit at once reverential and human' according to Alan Hull Walton. Burton's wife saw fit to burn the new edition upon which he was working when he died. *The Perfumed Garden* begins with these words: 'Praise be to God who has placed man's greatest pleasure in the natural parts of woman and has destined the natural parts of man to afford the greatest enjoyment of women.' In it is everything that is 'favourable to the act of coition' and much on aphrodisiacs from which the author of this book has been happy to borrow, as the Arabs had from India and the East.

India, which boasts a civilization five thousand years old, has a rich and artistic tradition of sexual lore. Whereas in the West today the body is often a source of shame in all but children, in Tantric India it is seen to be the vehicle by which knowledge is to be attained through ecstasy. Here the lingam (penis) and the yoni (female parts) are given their due respect and, long before the Romans raised their priapic statuary, were worshipped as symbols of fertility. Indian erotic painting and sculpture reflect a delight in the pleasures of the flesh as do the famous treatises on love, *The Ananga Ranga* of Kalyana and *The Kama Sutra* of Vatsyayana, valuable sources of information on aphrodisiacs and all things pertaining to love for both scholar and lover. The dedication to Kama, the Indian god of Love found in the beginning of *The Ananga Ranga* reveals the reverence accorded to love: 'Of charming sport, dweller in the hearts of all, destroyer of Sambara, solace to the eyes of Rati, of everlasting beauty, vanquisher of his enemies perforce, giver of bliss, to him – Kama, I bow.' *The Kama Sutra* gives many a recipe to increase sexual prowess: boiled asparagus and treacle in milk and ghee, spiced with liquorice; rice and sparrows' eggs cooked with honey, milk and ghee. *The Ananga Ranga* advises the lover to take a fudge made with ghee, sugar, honey and the juice of the *bhuya-kothali*. Other favourites for the Indian lover are onions, garlic, beans, honey and, heaven forbid, the flesh of owls and 'the soot which has been collected on a man's skull inverted on the burning pyre in the cremation grounds' – which, when applied to the eyes, will 'captivate the whole world'.

In China the stimulant taken orally was for the male alone, in order to condition his organ, while the female was encouraged by the external use of lotions and powders to excite her parts, as she was thought to need them less, the male arousal being more necessary to the sexual act. The commonest ingredients used were ginseng, cinnamon, seaweed, sulphur, pine needles, sea cucumber, the livers of various animals, sexual secretions and excreta, both human and from animals known for their power or predatory character like bears, goats and bulls. Sexual symbolism was very important to the Chinese. Animal horns, plants and fungi with penis-like shapes were popular. The Chinese were also aware of one of the most important aspects of the aphrodisiac, its influence on health and so on sex — 'nourishing' is a Chinese euphemism for aphrodisiac.

To reinforce the assault on the Jade Pavilion — one of the many poetic terms used in China for the sex act (the penis being the Jade Stalk or Stem, the female organ being the Jade Gate or Pavilion, and their conjunction known as the clouds and the rain) — the virile hero of the erotic book the *Chin P'ing Mei*, Hsi-men Ch-ing, obtained from an itinerant Tibetan monk an aphrodisiac pill. This he claimed would turn winter's night into spring morning:

> Which man would not prefer it to gold,
> Choose it rather than Jade,
> Exchange it for his silken robe,
> Or for his coat of finest sable?

Aphrodisiacs and love potions continued to enjoy brisk trade throughout nineteenth- and twentieth-century Europe and America where the tonics offered by quacks to pep up the lover were often the same concoctions which were used to restore the flagging powers of our ancestors. Now under the trade names of 'Zip', 'Passionettes', 'Make man' and 'Stifferene', these contained such things as vitamins, minerals, strychnine (see *Nux Vomica*), the dessicated testicles of animals (the so-called oysters) and other substances considered aphrodisiac by dint of their health-giving properties. 'Are you a Manly Man Full of Vigor?' they asked. Man has never been able to resist attractive labels. Even today, despite the Trade Descriptions Act, we are seduced into spending a fortune on cosmetic products which appear to compensate where nature has not been very generous. Equally simple faith in voodoo magic is found in the Southern states of America where negroes (and sensible whites) wishing for success in love or gambling carry 'Johnny the Conqueror' or 'High John the Conqueror' on their person. These are roots of the marsh St John's wort which has the additional virtue of protecting against all manner of evils. If the prong at the end of the root is short then the root is suitable for women and is then called 'Little John'. Men soak the root in sugar and go courting with it in their pocket and, according to Edward Gifford (in *The Charms of Love*), if the girl has already yielded but her passion for the man is cooling then the root must be dusted with pepper and sugar and placed under her bed when, 'She is gonna love you like you is never been loved'. A sympathetic wish, and one thing that the whole world shares, the desire for love.

An A–Z of Aphrodisiacs

A

ABSINTHE ♥♥♥

ABSINTHE WAS THE favourite tipple of the poets and painters of nineteenth-century France, especially the Impressionists who drank it to achieve an anxiety-free state where all the senses could combine together and they could transcend the conventions of classicism and interpret the world in terms of colour and light. This combination of wormwood, anise, marjoram and elecampane was narcotic and painkilling and most aphrodisiac, the principal chemicals responsible being absinthine and thujone. It was, however, the alcohol (ethanol) in absinthe that was the danger to health . . . the artistic souls who came to a sticky end by drinking it would not have been harmed by the thujone which although a poisonous substance was present in too small a proportion to prove lethal. It was probably the moral and revolutionary aspects of absinthe drinking that led to its being banned in many countries. Thujone is present in vermouth in legally permissible amounts. Six times this amount is needed to match the absinthe effect!

'The grape, more virtuous prior to fermentation.'

WHEN TAKEN WITH discretion, alcohol will relax the lover and remove the inhibitions. Too much alcohol will lead to loss of health and sexual vigour. More than a very modest amount will considerably impair sexual performance and will undoubtedly damage the liver and personality as well as deplete the body of its store of essential vitamins and minerals. Wine has often proved a convenient means of giving a love philtre to an unsuspecting victim but the drinks considered aphrodisiac in themselves are green Chartreuse, a liqueur containing Jamaican allspice among the other secret herbs, Strega, a veritable witches' brew from Italy, the apricot brandy Abricotine, Château Yquem, white port, champagne and of course vermouth (see *Absinthe*).

> Drinking wine by a mountain path
> I wave as she passes on pony back
> Pretty Maid of Wu, hardly fifteen
> I offer her the wine jar
> and she jumps down to drink with me
> Pretty Maid of Wu, hardly fifteen.
> Her manner bewitching, her eyes blue lined,
> She gets drunk on my lap
> Then yields to my passion
> O, that morning by a mountain path
> The warmth of the wine, and her caresses
> Pretty Maid of Wu, hardly fifteen.

LI PO, 8TH CENTURY CHINESE

ALMONDS ♥

ALTHOUGH NOT APHRODISIAC in the true sense of the word, almonds appear in aphrodisiac recipes and love potions the world over. These nuts are symbols of fertility and as such are given to guests at weddings and christenings in the Mediterranean countries. They are highly nutritious (the Chinese euphemism for aphrodisiac) having nearly twice the protein of beef. The almond has restorative properties and almond marzipan was suggested by Rabelais as a tonic and digestive. The almond broth given to the convalescent in a Victorian household could have been, with the addition of honey, recommended to the jaded Arabian lover. This was made by pounding blanched sweet almonds with milk or stock. If this does not appeal to today's lover then perhaps the eighteenth-century French recipe for 'eggs in moonshine' may tempt. Its every ingredient lays claim to being aphrodisiac. Beat together double cream with ground almonds, add rosewater to taste, then fold in stiffly beaten egg whites. Eat modestly.

AMBERGRIS ♥♥♥

AMBERGRIS IS A grey wax substance from the intestines of the cachalot or sperm whale, sometimes found floating in tropical seas. It has a strong, sweet, musky smell which is highly aphrodisiac and so is used in perfumery and amatory magic. It was the favourite scent of Madame du Barry and many a French eighteenth-century roué chewed lozenges of ambergris to sweeten the breath and increase the ardour. It is now prohibitively expensive but was formerly much used in festive cooking. Brillat-Savarin in his *Physiology of Taste* recommended a pint of hot chocolate with ambergris as a restorative – the very same that had made poor Madame de Pompadour so liverish and spotty. Brillat-Savarin had a friend who, anxious to prove himself to his younger and jealous wife, had exhausted himself to the point of impotence – he made him a broth containing onions, carrots, parsley, sugar and twenty grammes of powdered ambergris, with beef and the flesh of an old cock (sympathetic magic here!). This was to be taken every two hours. His ministrations were not in vain!

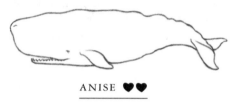

ANISE ♥♥

THE FRAGRANT SEEDS of the umbellifer *Pimpinella anisim*, a native of Egypt, are used in incense or with orris root in herbal sachets to perfume the person or the boudoir – anise is mildly stimulating and carminative. It was one of the main ingredients of a rich spiced cake served at Roman feasts – the origin of our wedding cake. Together with oil of wormwood and other herbs, anise is an ingredient of absinthe, the muse of many nineteenth-century poets and painters. An Indian recipe for enlarging the lingam (a common preoccupation) used powdered *shopa* (aniseed) softened in honey as an ointment to apply to the lingam before coitus. This was said to make a woman submissive to your will, so great would be her satisfaction.

BORN FROM THE foaming waters of the sea, the beautiful Aphrodite/Venus was worshipped by the Greeks as the goddess of both ideal and carnal love. In her role as Aphrodite Porne, the whore, she gave her name to the food and drugs inspiring sexual activity. The aphrodisiac may arouse desire, increase physical energy or enhance the act of love itself. It can do this in one or more of the following ways:

It may have a specific effect on the erogenous zones.

It may stimulate or act as an irritant, laxative or diuretic and focus the attention on the genital area.

It may stimulate the mind by suggestion or sexual symbolism.

It may relax both the body and the inhibitions.

It may be health-giving and nutritious and rich in vitamins and minerals.

It may prolong the act of love.

Aphrodisiacs may enhance, delight or inspire the mood as do lovely scents, beautiful music or delicious food and wine. The conditions under which aphrodisiacs are taken, all play their part. The atmosphere of the place of seduction is most important. Care must be taken as to the quantity. Too much of certain aphrodisiacs can at the very least impair digestion, and at the worst can kill — Madame de Pompadour was made ill by her own aphrodisiac preparations and many a Roman matron killed her lover by mistake with over enthusiastic use of poisonous aphrodisiacs — *venenum*, the Latin word for poison, was also the word for a love potion!

Sheikh Nefzawi in *The Perfumed Garden*, a must for students of aphrodisia, lists the 'causes of enjoyment' as 'bodily health, the absence of care and worry, an unembarrassed mind, natural gaiety of the spirit, good nourishment'.

APPLES ♥

THE FORBIDDEN FRUIT of the Garden of Eden was more highly esteemed in classical mythology where Juno gave the golden apples from the Garden of the Hesperides to Jupiter on their marriage, and the tricky Eris produced the golden apple which was to be awarded by Paris to the woman he judged to be the most beautiful, and in so doing sparked off the Trojan War. Apples were one of man's early foods and so an obvious symbol of fertility. They are tonic and act upon the sluggish liver. Sacred to Rhiannon, the Celtic Venus, apples have always been associated with love and marriage. To share an apple with a young man was thought to presage marriage to him.

Under her mother's nose
And avoiding her eye,
She slipped me a pair
Of apples; as she pressed
Them in my hands, love rose
And made me curse
Two apples in my grip
And not two breasts.

PAUL THE SILENTIARY, 6TH CENTURY

THE EGYPTIAN, THE Greek, the Roman and the Arab all delighted in the asparagus simply as a food or as an aphrodisiac. With the fall of the Roman Empire it disappeared along with many foods, the truffle among them, to appear again in medieval France thanks to Arab trade. In sixteenth-century England John Gerard says 'the young buds being steeped in wine and eaten, they stirreth up the lust of the body'. (Make sure that they are young as the old shoots have the reverse effect – this is surely sympathetic magic!) Culpeper writes that a 'decoction of the roots being taken fasting several mornings together, stirreth up bodily lust in man or woman' and he adds authoritatively 'whatever some have written to the contrary'! Asparagus is tonic to the urinary system and 'generally against all pains that happen to the lower part of the body' he says. Dipped in a sauce of melted butter, lemon juice and capers and eaten with the fingers, asparagus is a lovely feast indeed.

BANANA ♥♥♥

HERE PERHAPS IS a fine example of the doctrine of signatures whereby a clue to the properties of the plant is found in its appearance. The banana may have a suggestive shape and be nourishing in itself but, according to Dr Vernon Edwards, it is the alkaloid bufotenine in its skin which gives it its reputation as an aphrodisiac. This is a hallucinogen found in certain 'magic' mushrooms and the skin of the toads so beloved of witches. The most delicious way of obtaining this is by baking the banana and scraping out the inner skin. This recipe is aptly named 'black power'. Place as many ripe bananas as required in a baking dish and slit the skin lengthwise. Fill these cuts with sugar and bake them in a moderate oven for twenty minutes. Take them out and mix the juices with the inner scrapings from the skin. Pour over the bananas and serve with hot cream and Jamaican allspice.

BASIL ♥

'Woman is like a fruit, which will not yield its sweetness until you rub it between your hands. Look at the Basil plant; if you do not

rub it warm with your fingers it will not emit
any scent.'

SHEIKH NEFZAWI, THE PERFUMED GARDEN

IN THE WEST, many plants with fragrant flowers or
leaves were considered sacred to Venus and therefore
much used in amatory magic. A holy plant dedicated
to Venus and Krishna in India, whence it came, basil
has a clove-like fragrance which benefits the pot of
cook and witch alike. Basil leaf tea has soothing
properties. The herb marries beautifully with the egg
(see *Eggs*) and in conjunction with pine kernels makes
that delicate pesto sauce for pasta – not to be
overlooked or eschewed in the lover's kitchen.

Mix together:
1 cup pine nuts, coarsely grated
1 cup freshly grated Parmesan
1 cup whipped butter
8 large cloves garlic, peeled and crushed
2 teaspoons of salt
½ cup olive oil
2 cups basil leaves, chopped finely.

'Green peas boiled with onions and powdered
with cinnamon, ginger and cardamom, create
for the consumer amorous passion and
strength for coitus.'

THE PERFUMED GARDEN

A HEAVY MEAT diet has often been considered the stuff
of heroes. This is, however, justified only by its
bodybuilding protein content. It is the protein in
pulses that nourishes (without the attendant gout and
bowel disease) and places them among the aphrodisiacs. Beans, peas and lentils have always been
symbolic of fertility. Thus the broadbean provided
meat for feasting after funerals and assured the
continuance of life, hence the expression 'bean-feast'.
The smell of broadbean flowers is quite intoxicating.
Walk with your lover through a bean field in the heat
of the summer night and he or she will do your will.

Arabia cannot boast
a fuller gale of joy that liberal thence
Breathes through the sense and takes
the ravished soul.

Aristophanes, the Greek playwright, tells of an old
man with a young wife being restored to sexual
potency by a dish of lentils. Chickpeas are thought to
be most aphrodisiac – an Arabian poet tells us that
one 'Abu el Heidja had deflowered in one night once
eighty virgins and he did not eat or drink because he
surfeited himself first with chickpeas and had drunk

Camels milk with honey mixed.' Mediterranean
cultures lent aphrodisiacs to one another and so the
seventh-century physician Paul of Aegina might
concur with this.

BEE POLLEN ♥♥

Gay busy little tawny thing,
The herald of the sunny hours
Art mad with all the scent of Spring?

NICIAS OF MILETUS, GREECE, C. 300 B.C.

IF THERE IS anything that is guaranteed to give spring
fever then it is bee pollen. The Russians in 1946
concluded that the longevity and uncommon vitality
and virility of the bee keeper in Azerbaijan was due to
their eating honey scraps left by the bees. This was
almost pure bee pollen. Analysis reveals it to contain
small amounts of enzymes, hormones and aminoacids
among other foods, the combined effect of which is
most beneficial. Pollen as a dietary supplement taken
regularly is a true panacea for all ills, it stimulates the
regeneration of body tissues, restores vitality, increases resistance to infection, improves the tone of
skin and muscles and so cannot but be aphrodisiac.

THIS FISHY-TASTING soup is made from the nests of the sea-swallow (*salangane*) and is highly prized as aphrodisiac by the Chinese. The birds make them from edible seaweed glued together with fish spawn and their own saliva. The edible nest swiftlets living in the caves of Malaya and Indo-China make their nests entirely of strips of saliva. These nests are rich in phosphorus and are only for the very rich!

> Sweet girl not sixteen years
> Soft breasts white and smooth
> But between her legs a vicious trap
> That strikes at manly ardour.
> Hers is a cunning called passion
> For which man dies with pleasure
> His blood and essence drain away
> For that girl of sweet sixteen.

WANG SHIH-CHENG

CACTUS FLOWERS (*Cereus grandiflorus*)

THIS FLESHY SHRUB is found in the United States and
Mexico and parts of the Mediterranean. The large
white flowers bloom only for a night, giving off a
heady vanilla scent. They contain a powerful cardiac
stimulant which serves as a tonic in cases of sexual
fatigue. In her herbal, Mrs Grieve advises one to ten
drops of the extract. It is perhaps more sensible to
utilize the scent rather than the decoction which is a
potentially dangerous alkaloid and can cause internal
irritation and hallucinations.

CARAWAY

THE SEEDS OF this umbellifer contain an aromatic
essential oil. They are used in amatory magic and in
cooking to flavour pickles, cheeses and cakes. Caraway
seeds are considered aphrodisiac by association as they
promote the secretion of milk in nursing women.

> Display thy breasts, my Julia, there let me
> Behold that circummortal purity.
> Between those glories, there my lips I'll lay,
> Ravished, in that fair Via Lactea.

ROBERT HERRICK (1591–1674)

31

An Indian love charm instructs us to 'chew caraway seeds and with the mouth thus sweetened breathe on the beloved who will henceforth love you'.

CARDAMOM ♥

THIS SPICE IS tonic and a subtle aphrodisiac with a delectable taste. The ancient Arabs mixed it with saliva and spread it on the glans to excite the organ and increase its size. Cardamom can be used in love potions or amulets or in home cooking. Baked with apples in a pie and fed to the would-be lover they help to win his or her heart, it is said.

CARROTS ♥

THE CARROT IS sweet and nourishing with a suggestive length. They are mentally invigorating and restorative to the nervous system, and they are full of iron and vitamins (A, B and C). The Greeks called them *philon*, deriving from the word for loving, and served them to their lovers to excite them. Andrew Boorde, the English traveller and physician, wrote in his *Dyetary* (1542) that carrots 'increase nature'. Mixed with cardamom in carrot halva, they are a delicious Indian sweetmeat – appropriate food for lovers.

½ pint milk
1 lb grated carrots
3 oz soft brown sugar
1oz creamed coconut or butter

1oz ghee or butter
6 white cardamoms, skinned and crushed
1 dozen (approx.) blanched almonds

Boil the milk and carrots on a medium heat until the mixture thickens, stirring all the while. Add the sugar and the butter and cook until they are absorbed and the mix is thick like fudge. Turn this out on a plate and decorate with the almonds and cardamoms.

CELERY ♥

CELERY, LIKE TRUFFLES, contains a pig pheromone (see *Pheromones*). Since the likes of Madame de Pompadour would not have understood the significance of these chemicals they may have noted from observation and perhaps experience the aphrodisiac powers of celery soup.

CHAMPACA ♥

'Pale as the Champa flowers, violet veined that
sweet and fading lay in your loosened hair.'

LAWRENCE HOPE, THE GARDEN OF KAMA

A LOVELY FLOWER of the magnolia family, with a beautiful heavy scent, champaca is sacred to Vishnu and is used in potions and amulets in the East. Man has always known the relation between the olfactory and the sexual senses and has long employed perfumes to stimulate the opposite sex.

> 'The Semen of the healthy youths of western
> European races has a fresh exhilarating smell,
> in the mature man it is more penetrating in
> type and degree. The very characteristic
> seminal odour is remarkably like that of the
> flowers of the Spanish Chestnut.'

PROFESSOR GAMBER, *IDEAL MARRIAGE*

THE CHESTNUT BLOSSOM contains a combination of
chemicals also found in the seminal secretions of the
male, a heady draught for those of either persuasion —
Socrates taught his young men under its branches, de
Sade remarked upon its effect, which can be utilized
in scent or bath sachets . . . or visit Paris in late
spring when the chestnuts are in full bloom.

CIVET ♥♥♥

THIS FIERCE AND cat-like creature secretes a musky,
pungent substance from the glands in its rear. These
are periodically milked by its keeper (most profitably)
and the civet oil or tincture used in perfumes, incense
and love potions. It was the favourite scent of serious
eighteenth-century rakes!

CLOVES ❤

THE DRIED FLOWERS of the clove are ruled by Jupiter and are most stimulating. Used in cooking to flavour hot chocolate (*see* Cocoa) or apples or apricots and also in love potions. In India they are chewed to sweeten the breath before conversing with the loved one (or a Moghul emperor!).

COCOA ❤❤❤

'EVERY GIRL LIKES something hot inside her.' So said that paragon of Australian womanhood Dame Edna Everage. What better than a cup of hot chocolate? The waxy beans from the cocoa pod contain phenelethylamine (a mood-altering chemical which lends the body a feeling of post-coital bliss) and theobromine, a stimulant. The Aztecs thought cocoa to be the food of the gods (its Latin name *theobroma* means just that) given to men on earth by the god Quetzalcoatl. They prized it as a source of wisdom and courage giving strength and energy, and above all they used it as an aphrodisiac. Their king Montezuma II drank *xocoatl* (from which derives the word chocolate) from a golden cup as he sported with his harem of six hundred beauties. He is recorded as drinking up to fifty cups a day and making love to as many women. It was introduced in the eighteenth century to Europe by the Spanish conquistadores. Its use was then suppressed by the inquisition who did not share the Aztec view that this little luxury was sent from heaven. Madame du Barry the mistress of Louis XV fed her suitors with chocolate to increase their ardour. Both Casanova and the Marquis de Sade believed in its erotic properties. Today cocoa is seen by some researchers to be a mild genital tonic due to its diuretic action. Regrettably the lover needs an awful lot of cocoa to experience its aphrodisiac effect – a quarter of a pound of cocoa solids.

COCONUT ♥

IN HIS STUDY of magic and religion, *The Golden Bough*, Sir James Frazer writes that in upper India the coconut is esteemed one of the most sacred fruits, that of Sri, the goddess of Prosperity, and as such is symbolic of fertility and motherhood (one thing leading to the other), hence its use in Indian wedding ceremonies. Its flesh is fatty and nutritious and its milk a veritable *eau de vie*. Coconut milk with rum and Jamaican allspice will make you want to rock and roll – an obvious euphemism from black America!

CORIANDER ♥

CORIANDER SEEDS FEATURE in love potions by virtue of their lovely scent and flavour. The powdered seeds and fresh leaves are used in oriental cooking and are considered stimulant and digestive. It is amusing to note that in the Victorian *lingua flora* the coriander symbolized 'concealed merit'! There is a coriander love philtre, in use for a thousand years, which is made by grinding seven coriander seeds while naming the one the spell is to affect, and saying 'warm seed, warm heart, let them never be apart'. The powder is then steeped in spring water, strained and given to the lover mixed in his or her food or drink.

CUBEB ♥

SPICE WITH A faintly nutmeg flavour used in scent and incense for sensual effect. The Chinese and Arabs favour its use in love potions. The Arab, Abu Ali al Husain ibn Sina, a physician who was himself an example of loose living recommended chewing cubebs and spreading the resultant saliva on to the end of the male organ to increase the pleasure of both the male and the female when engaged in coitus (as with cardamom this might well be an irritant).

The heart of love can find no remedy
In witching sorcery nor amulets,
Nor in the fond embrace without a kiss,
Nor in a kiss without coitus.

ARABIAN WISDOM

DAMASK ROSE ♥

'THIS BARBERY ROSE seems to have thrown off its vegetable fragrance in favour of an animal scent,' and is, as are all roses, the symbolic attribute both of Diana, the mistress of the realms of Venus, and of the Queen of Heaven. Its petals can be strewn around the bedroom or used in a scent or amulet. A herbal bath-sachet can be made using rose petals and vervein tied in a muslin and then steeped in the hot bath water. 'In order to induce desire in the one you love add the resultant sweat from the body to a cake or wine and give it to the one you love' *Magiculture*.

DAMIANA (*Turnera aphrodisiaca*) ❤❤❤

A Mexican praying for love
Received some good news from above
With your Ave Maria
You must drink Damiana
Then you'll conquer your sweet turtle dove.

THE LEAVES OF this small shrub have been used for centuries in Mexico and tropical South America as an aphrodisiac. Damiana justifies its reputation acting as a gentle purge and mildly irritating the genito-urinary tract which stimulates the sexual parts. It produces a euphoric state not unlike marijuana. One ounce of damiana leaves infused in a bottle of tequila for a week will make a veritable love potion relaxing the inhibitions and concentrating the attention on the appropriate parts. A tea can be made of two heaped tablespoons steeped in a cup of boiling water for five minutes, then strained. This is aromatic but bitter so improve the taste with honey.

DITA ❤❤❤

THE SEEDS OF the dita tree have long been used in India as an aphrodisiac. They contain an allergin chlorogenic acid which irritates the urinary system and causes a sweet tingling in the genitals. They are stimulating and a general tonic. *The Ananga Ranga* advises that 'the seeds collected from the tree on Sunday, kept in the mouth during sexual union long retain the seminal fluid of men'. Miller in his *Magical Use of Aphrodisiacs* advises soaking two grammes of crushed seed in two fluid ounces of water at night. The liquid is then strained and drunk the next day. As with all alkaloids care must be taken as to the individual's tolerance.

The heart is no heart if not a fireplace
The breath is no breath if not a volcano.

GHALIB (1797—1869)

EGGS

Fain would I kiss my Julia's dainty legg,
Which is as white and hairless as an egg.

ROBERT HERRICK

ALL EGGS INCLUDING caviar (sturgeons' eggs), snails'
eggs and sperm, both human and animal (long
considered to be aphrodisiac in the East) are universal
symbols of fertility, procreation and new life; they are
nutritious and their restorative value has been made
use of in aphrodisiac recipes throughout the centuries.
Dr Lorand in his *Health and Longevity through Rational
Diet* says this:

> Other articles of diet, particularly eggs and
> caviar, are also supposed to exert a stimulating
> action upon sexual activity. It is customary to
> say, *vox populi vox Dei*, and as far as foods are
> concerned I would be inclined to consider that
> in the case of such empiric beliefs, which have
> been handed down to us from time immemorial,
> even medical science – which has undoubtedly
> frequently profited by such statements – should
> not pass them by without notice . . . It
> seems to me quite certain that a plentiful diet

containing, in particular, much protein would have an exciting influence upon the sexual function.

The revered Sheikh Nefzawi says: 'He who makes it a practice to eat every day fasting [by this one supposes he means for breakfast] the yolk of eggs, without the white part, will find in this aliment an energetic stimulant for coitus.' A friend of mine knew a German lady in Cairo who always insisted that he ate four raw eggs before he visited her.

Many an English colonel will attest to the properties of an egg flip:

4 egg yolks
4 oz caster sugar
¼ pint Marsala

Put the yolks together with the sugar and Marsala into a basin over a pan of simmering water. Whisk until thick and foaming. Pour into individual glasses and serve warm.

ENDIVE ♥

'And none but thou shall be my paramour.'

CHRISTOPHER MARLOW, DR FAUSTUS

A FREQUENT INGREDIENT in old love philtres, succory (as endive was also known) was said to ensure constancy in love. It is certainly on the side of the angels for it is tonic, restorative and invigorating, and purges the body of impurities.

ERYNGO ♥

NICHOLAS CULPEPER's *Complete Herbal* tells us that the common eryngo or sea-holly is venereal, and 'breeds seed exceedingly, and strengthens the spirit procreative; it is hot and moist, and under the celestial balance'. In Shakespeare's time 'kissing comforts' made from Spanish sweet potatoes and eryngo roots were much enjoyed, but for the maiden wishing to preserve her chastity 'eryngoes are not good for to be taken'.

Her slender arms, her soft and subtle back,
Her tapered sides – all fleshy smooth and white
He stroked, and asked her favours at her neck,
Her snowish throat, her breasts so round and
     light,
Thus in this heaven he took his delight,
and smothered her with kisses upon kisses,
Till gradually he come to learn where bliss is.

GEOFFREY CHAUCER, TROILUS AND CRISEYDE

THE SPANISH FLY (*Cantharides*) and iron filings fed to the youthful Louis XIV by his mistress Madame de Montespan may well have turned him into a satyr (and served the interests of his other mistresses to boot) but it was his daily exercise of hunting and shooting that kept him healthy in his seventies. His poor wife Madame de Maintenon found his twice daily love-making to be most tiring at her age. Exercise strengthens, tones and regulates the body and stimulates the mind. It relieves tensions, aids digestion and improves the figure. It raises the beta endorphin level in the blood which may be responsible for an elevated mood. In short, it creates harmony throughout the whole body.

> With a harmonious spirit the Jade stem will
>   always stiffen,
> With a mood that is dark and bitter, it is like a
>   thorn piercing one's own flesh.

SU NU CHING, *CONVERSATIONS BETWEEN THE YELLOW
EMPEROR HUANG TI AND THE WISE MAIDEN*

The Ananga Ranga, the great Indian treatise on love, states that having exhausted the body by sports or amusements, a woman possessed of passion will usually reach her climax easily. Remembering the birth of Venus, swimming may well be the best exercise to serve your ends. It strengthens every muscle, stimulates the circulation of the blood and relaxes tension. The dreadful Roman Emperor Tiberius, who was too far gone in his debauchery to benefit from normal healthy exercises himself, trained little boys to swim around him in the pool and nibble him. To improve the female muscle control, here is a good exercise to do in or out of water: Tighten the thighs and the muscles of the nether regions, hold for four seconds and relax. Repeat this ten times daily. It can then be applied most satisfactorily when love-making.

FASTING ♥♥

MANY APHRODISIAC RECIPES recommend that the lover take them 'whilst fasting' when the senses are heightened. Any food eaten then raises the blood sugar in order to give the lover energy for congress. Fasting invigorates and purifies the body and is held to be the cure for many ills. In the East it is almost always the preliminary to ritual undertakings. Sheikh Nefzawi in *The Perfumed Garden* warns us that 'fasting if prolonged calms the sexual desires but in the beginning it excites them'. Still less can one enjoy the pleasures of the senses sated with too much food and alcohol, when 'venereous acts doth engender the cramps, the gout and other displeasures'. Ovid warns us to eat 'somewhat less than we are able for if Paris saw Helen eating greedily he should deem his prize a foolish woman'. The following three-day diet beginning with a fast will purge the body of impurities and leave the lover full of energy. To maintain vigour and vitality the diet includes eighty per cent raw fruit and vegetable matter which clears toxins and provides minerals and vitamins otherwise washed out by cooking, and of course provides essential roughage. Because of its revitalizing, nerve-restoring and antiseptic qualities carrot juice is all that is taken on the first day to obviate the more tiresome effects of fasting.

1st day	carrot juice and mineral water
2nd day	
breakfast:	freshly squeezed orange juice and a tablespoonful of safflower oil; muesli with wheatgerm and sesame seeds
mid-morning:	carrot juice
lunch:	finely sliced vegetables (carrots, cabbage, tomato, watercress, fennel, broccoli, spring onions) with avocado dip (mashed avocado, lemon juice and cottage cheese blended together)
tea:	tea or carrot juice
supper:	buckwheat spaghetti with sauce made from sieved fresh tomatoes and a quarter of an onion chopped with fresh basil and half a tablespoon of olive oil. Heat but do not cook
3rd day	
breakfast:	freshly squeezed orange and a tablespoonful of safflower oil. 2 boiled free-range eggs and wholemeal bread. No butter or margarine
mid-morning:	carrot juice
lunch:	salad of ricotta and walnuts, blanched broccoli, tomato
tea:	tea or carrot juice
supper:	1 baked potato with sweet corn and yoghurt filling, green beans lightly cooked; banana

Drink as much mineral water as you require up to one litre a day. No salt. No coffee. Weak tea with lemon

and half a teaspoon of honey if you feel cold or in need
of it.

FENNEL ♥♥

FENNEL IS SAID to give a delicious itch to those who eat
it. It has a fragrance like anise containing as it does
the same essential oil, anethol. It gently stimulates
the digestion and is diuretic . . . as such it focuses
upon the nether regions reminding the body of its
loving function. Fennel has a thick white rootstock
from which spring branches with tiny delicate green
leaves. The Italian name for fennel, *finnocchio*, is also
given to the perversely elegant homosexual. The
gladiators of ancient Rome were seen as symbols of
virility and idolized as are the stars of screen and stage
today. They were given fennel everyday to increase
their valour, as in Love's battle.

It gave new strength and fearless mood;
And gladiators, fierce and rude,
Mingled it with their daily food;
And he who battled and subdued,
A wreath of fennel wore.

LONGFELLOW, 'THE GOBLET OF LIFE'

An infusion of vervein and fennel gathered on a
Friday, the day dedicated to Venus, is said to fill the
lover with desire.

FIGS ♥

FIGS ARE A fruit assigned to Pan which, when slit
open, are suggestively venereal; remember Alan Bates
in the picnic scene in Ken Russell's film of D. H.
Lawrence's *Women in Love*. Both Greeks and Romans
thought them to be aphrodisiac . . . they certainly
stimulate the digestive process and relieve the
sluggish system. Figs contain potassium.

Stewed figs in garlic may appear bizarre but this
recipe makes a delightful end to a cosy meal *à deux*:

1 lb fresh figs
2 glasses red wine
½ pint of crème fraîche or single cream
3 tblsp of honey
½ tsp thyme
½ tsp lavender
1 clove of garlic

Simmer all the ingredients in a covered saucepan for an hour, turning the figs occasionally. Remove the figs to a serving dish, sieve out the thyme and lavender and the garlic and reduce the liquid to the consistency of syrup. Pour this over the figs. Chill and serve with cream.

FO-TI-TIENG (*Hydrocotyle asiatic minor*)

A DAILY DRINK of half a teaspoonful of powdered fo-ti-tieng in hot water will condition the body, calm the nerves, increase energy and mental alacrity and soften the signs of ageing — a daily tablespoon of fo-ti-tieng will act as a sexual stimulant. It is, however, narcotic in too large a dose. The Indians and Singhalese who know it as *gotu kola* recommend 'two fresh leaves a day to keep old age away'. In China this creeping perennial herb was known as the 'elixir of long life'. The Chinese also made much of its revitalizing and restorative power. It encourages the women's courses. Teng-Tsi-Tsieng, in the Ming period, wrote that 'the beneficial fluid lies in the flowery pavilion when the gate is closed, and only flows once the woman is excited by intercourse. To draw the vital essence into himself, the man must press in fiercely but withdraw slowly, so dragging it into the skin of the male peak. Those who nourish themselves on these medicines will know the full pleasure of serenity. Their fiercest desires will be enjoyed calmly, those whose hair has turned grey will find it restored to black, and those who have grown old will again enjoy the joys of youth.'

GARLIC

Scorn not garlic like some that think
It only maketh men wink and drink and stink.

SIR JOHN HARRINGTON, 1609

GARLIC PROMOTES HEALTH, is a diuretic, antibacterial agent and a 'hot food'. With these properties the ancient Jews read the garlic as magic and a charm against the plague. They cultivated it as a staple food and their rabbis instructed them to eat garlic on Friday (the eve of the Sabbath and, by coincidence, the day dedicated to Venus) to enliven the marriage bed, for they held the garlic in high esteem as an aphrodisiac, as did the Romans later, when at their orgiastic banquets the citizens ate quantities of garlic.

Pliny tells us that 'garlic . . . beaten up with fresh coriander, and taken in pure wine' acts as an aphrodisiac. Strict Hindus abhorred the use of garlic which distracted from the spiritual life; in China the Buddhist priesthood was banned from eating it. Mediterranean nations have always been great garlic eaters which may be the reason for their reputation as great lovers! The Victorians thought it vulgar to eat garlic, perhaps they feared its influence on propriety. 'The stinking rose', however, has one drawback – an anti-social smell for which there is only one real antidote (though some advise chewing parsley or cardamom) – that is to make sure that you are not alone in eating it, lest your lover 'push away your kisses and flee far from you' (Horace).

GINGER (*Zingiber*) ❤

The night to the furthest corner
is filled with our embrace
Why should I call for lotus wine,
When I am drinking her fiery breath.

FANN FANN CHAN

THE GINGER ROOT, familiar to the Chinese cook, is also valued as an aphrodisiac in the West. Its irritant effect will stir the fires of passion very nicely. An ointment of ginger mixed with pellitory of Spain and lilac oil, or simply honey, when rubbed on the already throbbing shaft will greatly increase its size, the Arabs claimed (the resultant inflammation may be more than was desired).

FIVE THOUSAND YEARS ago the Chinese Emperor Shen Nung praised Ginseng as a tonic ministering to the mind, the body and the spirit. In India the Atharva Veda extols it as an aphrodisiac. It is an adaptogen, that is to say it appears to make good any deficiencies in the system. Research in Russia has shown it to perk up Russian workers' appetites and increase their output by ten per cent when they are regularly dosed with ginseng. It appears to stimulate the metabolism as a whole and according to Dr Brekhman of the USSR: 'It stimulates both mental and physical activity and strengthens and protects the human organism.' In the early eighteenth century a Jesuit missionary working in Canada identified the wild ginseng used by the American Indians as an aphrodisiac to be the same as that used by the Chinese who called it 'jen shen' meaning 'man-root' due to its root being shaped like a human body. They held it in great esteem for its health-giving and aphrodisiac properties and dubbed it the 'king of all herbs'. Wild ginseng root is today most highly prized and worth many times more than its weight in gold. This panacea for all ills has now been cultivated for more than four hundred years – it takes six to seven years to grow to maturity and in so doing it absorbs so many valuable elements and nutrients that the soil must rest for ten years before the next crop is sown.

GOLD ♥♥

GOLD, THE SYMBOL of power and success, buys luxury, and comfort and the leisure to enjoy life, this we know. It allows the rich the freedom to choose a healthier way of life – for health and wealth are always linked in wishful thinking. Gold, it almost seems unnecessary to say, is an attractant and an aphrodisiac (old rich men with failing powers take heart!). *The Ananga Ranga* cites gold and its preparations as 'a nervine and aphrodisiac tonic, resolvent and alternative. They are said to increase strength and beauty, improve intellect and memory, clear the voice and increase sexual power. They also increase the flow of menses in women.' In ancient Rome an amulet of gold or lead in the shape of a phallus was a sovereign charm for a successful love-life, with, it must be added cautiously, a fertile outcome!

GUARANA (*Paullinia cupana*) ❤❤❤

THE FLESH-COLOURED seeds of this climbing shrub from the tropical jungles of South America are roasted and ground into a powder then mixed with water and rolled into sticks which serve the Amazonian Indians as a substitute for food when on hunting expeditions. It sharpens the mind and enables the user to remain awake while slowing the pulse rate and suppressing hunger – it does, however, stimulate the sexual appetite. (*See* Fasting.)

HEMP ♥♥

HASHISH, KNOWN TO the Arabs as 'the increaser of pleasure', is the resin extracted from the hemp plant (*Cannabis sativa* or *indica*) which grows wild in Asia Minor and northern India as well as along the Mississippi-Missouri basin. It is considered aphrodisiac by virtue of its relaxing sedative effect. It opens sensual and sexual awareness. Alice B. Toklas says that it gives 'extensions of the personality on several simultaneous planes'. Although it is said to remove inhibitions its 'volume-control' effect can turn up or down, and any feelings of sexual inadequacy can be intensified. Its seeds are used in love potions and witches have traditionally used hemp in flying ointments (Freudian n'est ce pas?). Note that its use is not universally legal so appropriate respect should be paid to the laws of the land.

HONEY ♥

Melissa, you are just like your namesake, the
    honey bee. I know this and take it to heart.
    When you kiss so sweetly, honey drips from
    your lips. When you ask for your fee, how
    you sting me.

MARCUS ARGENTARIUS TO THE PROSTITUTE MELISSA

THROUGHOUT THE ANCIENT world and up until today honey features in aphrodisiac cookery and ointments. In Oriental, Arab, Greek, Roman and Indian literature honey is used as a medium for mixing with herbs and spices, being sweetening, sticky and delicious, and in itself, according to Miss Barbara Cartland (and generations of lovers before her), a powerful aphrodisiac. It was thought, like salt, to strengthen and lengthen the effect of love potions and spells. It is an energy food and valuable in preventing inflammation in wounds – no germs can live in honey.

If you know how to approach her
She will mix every night, her honey with your
milk.

JAPANESE SAYING

HUMOUR ♥

Let us have wine and women, mirth and
laughter,
Sermons and soda water the day after.

LORD BYRON

IN *The Perfumed Garden* Sheikh Nefzawi cites as one of the 'causes of enjoyment' natural gaiety of the spirit. This is a most attractive quality in a lover. Madame de Pompadour the mistress of Louis XV of France, Nell Gwynne the 'pretty witty Nell' of Charles II of England and many famous lovers of history have all been vivacious and warm-hearted. Casanova, said to be the greatest lover of all time, had the ability to make his ladies laugh. They might otherwise have found his suspicious nature and his reputation daunting (he claimed to have had over 1,500 women), but laughter soon dispels anxiety.

HYACINTH ♥

THE PERFUME OF this flower fills the senses with a yearning for love, an effect perhaps endorsed by its phallic shape. It was said to have sprung from the blood of Hyacinthus, the favourite of Apollo and the brother of Diana, who was killed while sporting with the discus — thus the hyacinth is the emblem of play and games. Leland in his *Gypsy Sorcery* gives an enchanting little ritual:

> Plant a hyacinth bulb in a pot, name it for your loved one and every morning and evening as you water it chant over it these words: 'As the root grows and the blossoms blows. May thy heart be turned to me. As my will so mote it be.'

J

JASMINE 💜

In spring the natural friend of the young
Charming with fragrance of Madhavika
And the jasmine scent, overpowering,
Swaying with folly the minds even of the sages.

THE SONG OF LOVE, TRANSLATED FROM THE SANSKRIT
BY GEORGE KEYT

THE EXQUISITE JASMINE with its delicate white flowers
is known in India as 'Moonlight of the grove'. The
intoxicating scent sweetens the night air of both
tropical and temperate climes. It is uplifting, euphoric and relaxing to the body, and therefore the
perfect constituent of many a love philtre. In *The
Ananga Ranga* we are advised to apply it as a poultice

to the loins or mons veneris as an aprodisiac. To create an atmosphere conducive to love, the room may be scented by an aromatic candle made by adding a few drops of the essential oil of jasmine to melted wax. This is then poured over a domestic candle suspended by its wick until it is thoroughly coated.

There is a thing which in the light
Is seldom used, but in the night
It serves the Maiden female crew
The Ladies, and the good-wives too.

'THE CANDLE', SIR JOHN SUCKLING (1609—42)

KAVA KAVA (*Piper methysticum*)

A DRINK MADE from the masticated root of the kava kava mixed with coconut milk is taken as a ritual sacrament by the islanders of the Pacific. It is narcotic and generates feelings of warmth and camaraderie and tranquillity which can transmute into an aphrodisiac effect. The mind, however, remains clear and the user may hallucinate. One teaspoon of the powdered root will produce euphoria, more than that will induce sleep (not perhaps the intention) and too great an amount will paralyse.

L

LADY'S BEDSTRAW (*Galium verum*) ♥♥

DIOSCORIDES SAITH: '. . . ye root doth provoke to conjunction.' Lady's bedstraw is so named on account of its honey-scented odour and golden flowers. An infusion of thirty grammes of the dried leaves in a litre of water, three cups taken between meals, daily, will soothe the nervous and be diuretic, clearly under Venus's dominion.

LIQUORICE ♥♥

> 'This plant is born of honey, with honey do we
>   dig for thee. Of honey thou art begotten, do
>   thou make us full of honey.'

THE ATHARVA-VEDA

THE PEELED ROOT of the sweet wood or liquorice growing in Arabia, Persia and Indian gardens is used in aphrodisiacs chiefly because of its laxative effect and because it is said to be a sovereign cure for disorders of the womb, the seat of Venus. (Among other things it contains oestrogen.) It also raises the blood pressure due to sodium retention in the kidneys (*see* Nicotine).

He who having taken a Karsha [280 grammes Troy weight] of liquorice, drinks after it the cow's milk mixed with honey and ghee [clarified butter] would feel himself a hundred fold sexually strong.

THE ANANGA RANGA

LOVE MAGIC

WHEN THE LOVER is doubtful of his ability to win the affections of the beloved then he may seek the unconditional love promised by amatory magic. From ancient times until today the lover has resorted to the use of magic as a means of obtaining love or sexual power over the object of his desires. This can be sympathetic magic where the ingredients of ritual, spell or charm are obtained from animals or herbs considered to be particularly beautiful, prolific or amorous by nature or the substances used may indeed have aphrodisiac properties. Reinforced by magic these may be introduced into drink or food. They may be worn as an amulet or talisman or buried under the would-be lover's doorstep over which he has to pass . . . the methods are legion, but whichever is adopted be sure that a hint to the victim will strengthen the effect! Edward Gifford in his delightful *The Charms of Love* points out that 'the popularity and longevity of a belief bear witness, not to its truth, but to a universal desire to believe it true'. But who are we to say that this is all there is to magic?

MANDRAKE (*Mandragora officianarum*)

THE MANDRAGORA OFFICIANARUM is a purple flowering plant of the potato family which is native to the Mediterranean countries. Both its orange fruit and forked fleshy roots are used in amatory magic. Mandrake contains parasympathetic depressants and is rich in mandragorine, a powerful hypnotic hallucinogen. It induces a dreamlike state during which the lover might indulge in sexual fantasies – or the witch go riding on her broomstick, for it was one of the principal ingredients of 'flying spells'! It is extremely toxic and best left alone. The forked roots of this plant, when carved to resemble little mannikins, were prized as amatory talismans and amulets. They are said to shriek most frightfully when pulled up from the ground and kill the hapless man attempting this — far better to sacrifice your dog to this dangerous task, for which you will be fully compensated by the many magical properties of the mandrake: it ensures fertility and prevents impotence when simply carried on the person.

MASSAGE ♥♥♥

'The Serpent rises'

THIS IS THE name so aptly given to the oriental massage technique used to encourage the weary male member: sit astride the back of the man and press the thumbs hard into the indentations in the back approximately two inches down from the waist and from the backbone. The tips of the fingers meanwhile exert a gentle pressure into the hollows between the hips and bottom. Rhythmic movements will slowly restore him to manhood.

Here are some variations for moving the 'Jade thrusting Root' from *The Ying-Yang: The Chinese Way of Love*:

1. Float and sink in the same movement, like a duck on the ripples of a lake
2. Peck like a sparrow with rice seeds, now deep, now shallow
3. A slow movement like a snake entering its hole to hibernate.

When your lingam becomes as hard as the
    poised cobra,
make sure that all the holes in your flute are
    stopped
so as not to break the spell.

TANTRA

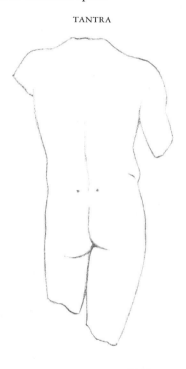

MUSHROOMS ♥♥

ACCORDING TO THE doctrine of signatures the
mushroom should certainly be aphrodisiac for, in its
raw state, it gives off a smell of sex redolent of the
lover's bedroom. Sheuer in his *Alphabet of Sex* includes

the mushroom (especially the morel) 'for illuminating once again suitable desire and ability'. The Greeks and Romans would agree. Along with its inspiring odour come a wide range of vitamins, trace elements and protein.

MUSK ♥♥♥

THIS IS THE sexual attractant which is produced by a gland beneath the abdomen of the male musk deer. Musk is found in many Chinese, Indian and Persian medicines and love potions and is used as a fixative and scent in perfumery. It is mixed with honey and hemp seeds in India as an aphrodisiac sweetmeat and combined with frankincense, myrrh, camphor and rosewater in ointment to rub on Arab loins.

It appears in Ayurvedic (Hindu) and Chinese medicine as a virtual panacea – it acts both as a sedative and a stimulant to the heart and nervous system. It calms the senses and yet arouses animal desire. In China the deer are now raised in semi-captivity and the musk extracted annually to obviate the traditional slaughter by gun, snare and poison. It is hoped that this method will prove universally successful, for musk is the world's most expensive animal product and the survival of the musk deer is a matter of grave concern to conservationists, according to the World Wildlife Fund.

NETTLES ♥

FULL OF IRON for vigour and crammed with vitamins and other minerals, the tonic properties of nettles are well thought of. Pepper ground with nettle seed and bunches of its leaves have whipped up the ardour of the flagging male from Roman times to those of Casanova. In the *Satyricon* of Petronius the hero, having failed to enlist the aid of Priapus to cure his impotence, resorts to these painful means and ends up running through the streets of Rome crying in agony rather than with ecstasy. 'For the erection of the yeard to synne' the seventeenth-century gallant was advised to put nettles in his cod-piece. With less discomfort we might eat the nettle stewed with milk and nutmeg as in this recipe. The sting is neutralized by cooking.

Glaze a chopped onion in butter. Add to this three large handfuls of nettles (washed with care!). These will reduce in the pan. Steam for three minutes in the water remaining on the leaves. Add a pint of milk with half a pint of stock and bring nearly to boiling point. Take from the heat and liquidize the whole. Season with salt, pepper and nutmeg.

The nettle was thought to provide protection against sorcery, growing as it did beside the entrances of faery dwellings. The seeds were therefore useful in an amulet to ensure no witch would render impotent the lover. Sir Richard Burton tells us the Arabs take nettle seed in honey as a cure for impotence 'with the permission of God the Highest!'

NUTMEG ♥♥

THE SEED OF the nutmeg tree is ruled by Jupiter and so is considered soothing, benevolent and jovial. Its outer envelope is the less pungent mace. Used in cooking and spicy scents it contains a hallucinogenic amphetamine, methylenedioxyamphetamine. Do not, however, be alarmed as the amount needed to cause hallucinations would be unacceptable to the palate. There is, however, a harmless combination found in a book on aphrodisiacs by Dr Edward Vernon. A quarter of an ounce of grated nutmeg is mashed with half an avocado pear and chilled for twenty-four hours. The chemical in the nutmeg reacts with the bromocriptine in the pear (a chemical increasing the sex drive in the male) releasing its sexually stimulating effect. This will serve to improve the ardour only of the male; the female may benefit but indirectly.

NUX VOMICA ♥♥♥

NUX VOMICA IS a preparation made from strychnine. In homeopathic doses it is tonic and aphrodisiac . . . it stimulates the nerves in the backbone and encourages peristalsis. Purges have always been considered useful in restoring the lover to form – Casanova was a great believer in them (*see* Fasting). Used in conjunction with damiana, nux vomica rarely fails.

ONIONS ♥♥

The member of Abou el Heloukh has remained
   erect,
For thirty days without a break because he did
   eat onions

THE PERFUMED GARDEN

RULED BY MARS, the god of War, and given by
Alexander the Great to encourage his troops, the
onion is nutritious and mildly purgative. Onions were
said by Culpeper to 'increase sperm and provoke
women's courses' – anything which is associated with
the procreative purpose is considered aphrodisiac as
we have seen. In the *Remedia Amores* Ovid advises the
disappointed lover wishing to forget his unrequited
love not to fuel his passion by eating onions. The
Egyptians banned their priests from eating onions.
Devout Hindus were forbidden to eat onions as they
were seen to hinder self-control. So those aspiring to
spirituality were to avoid the onion, but others with
more carnal goals advised to eat it . . . spiced with
ginger, cinnamon and cardamom in Arabia, fried in
ghee in Indian, 'Boyled' in Stuart England, or eaten as
onion soup in France today.

This following recipe for 'energy' soup will act as a
restorative to the lover. In some regions of France this
was taken to a young couple after their wedding

night. Glaze two large onions in butter. Pour over them a pint of milk and bring to the boil. Remove and liquidize. Add an egg and further liquidize. Season with salt and pepper. Sheik Nefzawi would approve!

OYSTERS ♥♥

NOT ONLY DO oysters come like Venus from the sea, but they resemble sympathetically the female genitalia and are a most healthy food full of phosphorus, zinc and copper (*see* Vitamins and Minerals) to nourish the body and the brain. The Greeks and Romans knew the pleasures of eating oysters and rated them most aphrodisiac. Oysters sent from Colchester to Rome were consumed in enormous quantities – the Emperor Vitellius once ate as many as a thousand at one sitting! Whereas today they are thought to be a luxury, the London poor of Dickens's time would have had an even harder battle for survival had it not been for the cheapness of oysters. John Rydon in his amusing book *Oysters with Love* gives a recipe for *croquettes d'huitres* which is adapted here:

Poach as many oysters as are needed and dice them up. Mix them with béchamel sauce to which has been added the reduced liquor from the oysters bound with yolk of egg. After cooling, shape the mixture into croquettes, dip them in egg and breadcrumbs and fry in very hot fat. Serve garnished with parsley.

(Salsify is a vegetable with long fleshy roots known as the vegetable oyster. Boiled, then creamed with butter and milk, and seasoned with salt, pepper and lemon juice, this is simply delicious with a distinct oyster flavour.)

PEACHES ♥

THIS ROUND AND luscious juicy fruit with a suggestive shape was the ambrosia of the Chinese gods. Peaches were considered aphrodisiac by the Stuarts — certainly inspiring to James I! In India a Pushti poet of the homosexual persuasion wrote these amusing lines: 'The boy across the river has a bottom like a peach, but how can I get to him whilst the water's in full flood?'

PEPPER ♥

BOTH BLACK AND white pepper come from the same berry, the white is the inner fruit minus its black husk, and is less pungent than the black. Pepper was once so highly prized that when the Goths were besieging Rome the ransom paid was in peppercorns. It is stimulating and tones the muscles, so perhaps deserves a little of its reputation as an aphrodisiac.

PHEROMONES ♥♥♥

PHEROMONES ARE CHEMICALS made by the body as sexual attractants. In the human being they are produced at the root of the hair follicles under the arm and around the groin. They are unique to the individual and along with the more personal attributes they contribute to the sexual charisma. The female pheromones act as male erectants and male pheromones moisturize the female. They can be detected by the olfactory senses but their message is largely to the subconscious. They could possibly be a great asset to the perfume industry, considerably enhancing the reputation of some scents – their use is however banned in many American states as a violation of civil rights, for the individual might not be able to control his impulses in response to them!

PINE KERNELS ♥

IN HIS *De Arte Amoris*, Ovid advised eating the 'nuts upon the sharp-leaved pine trees growing'. These nutritious pine kernels from the woods and forests where Pan was wont to frolic were dedicated to him by the Romans and considered to be a powerful aphrodisiac. Given the nature of their pantheistic festivities, anything associated with this goat-limbed deity would doubtless have inspired the Romans to lasciviousness, for during these feasts intended to ensure fertility, behaviour was unrestrained to say the least. The participants, drunken and drugged, launched themselves upon one another in unbridled lust . . .

PORNOGRAPHY

THIS EXTRACT FROM *Under the Hill* by Aubrey
Beardsley, a work of exquisite and decadent eroticism,
describes how the Chevalier Tannhauser entered into
the Hill of Venus:

The place where he stood waved drowsily with
strange flowers, heavy with perfume, dripping
with odours. Gloomy and nameless weeds not to
be found in Mentzelius. Huge moths, so richly
winged they must have banqueted upon tapes-
tries and royal stuffs, slept on the pillars that

flanked either side of the gateway, and the eyes of all the moths remained open and were burning and bursting with a mesh of veins. The pillars were fashioned in some pale stone and rose up like hymns in the praise of pleasure, for from cap to base, each one was carved with loving sculptures, showing such a cunning invention and such a curious knowledge, that Tannhauser lingered not a little in reviewing them. They surpassed all that Japan has ever pictured in her maison vertes, all that was ever painted in the cool bath-rooms of Cardinal La Motte.

Since early times books have been written and illustrated to stimulate the sexual passions – the word pornography means literally 'harlots' tales'. These range from the bawdy stories of Petronius and Boccaccio to the works of Sacher-Masoch and de Sade, from Indian and Arabian manuals on love to the extensive erotic literature of China and Japan. Some of these books are quite delightful while others disgust and shame the reader. The question is whether or not pornography corrupts – in Denmark when the ban on pornographic literature was lifted sexually related crimes did not increase, and certain of them acutally decreased. It appears therefore to be a question of moral values.

PRUNES ♥

THE DRIED FRUITS of the *Prunus domestica* are an excellent energy food and as such were fed to the clients of Elizabethan brothels. They are, however, more often taken as a cure for a sluggish constitution. A soothing antidote to irritability, the Victorians considered them to be a remedy for viciousness.

PUMPKIN SEEDS ♥

RESTORATIVE AND RICH in protein, zinc and other minerals essential to the sexual function, these were formerly taken to quieten the ardour but are now restored to favour.

PUSSYWILLOW BARK (*Salyx nigra*) ♥♥♥

THE BARK OF this ornamental tree with its amusing little catkins hinting of its virtues, contains tannin and salinigrin, a glucoside with tonic, sedative and aphrodisiac properties. Mrs Grieve's *Modern Herbal* recommends half a teaspoon of the fluid extract.

RHINO HORN

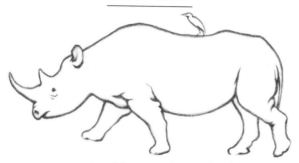

THE HORN OF the rhinoceros is, to the detriment of the species, a phallic symbol. For centuries powdered rhino horn has been prized as aphrodisiac by the orientals. Three thousand years ago the Chinese Emperor Chou-Hsin, the dragon lover, a man so virile that he fought wild animals bare-handed and would balance a naked woman on his erect member for the amusement of his court, was faced with impotence. To restore his prowess he resorted to an aphrodisiac brew, the so-named 'hunting lion' containing stewed bear's paw flavoured with ground rhino horn (*shi-ngiu-chiao*) and distilled urine. Rhinoceros horn is, however, no real aphrodisiac but its use is sympathetic magic, for the horn (or rather hair, for that is what it is) contains little more than traces of minerals and for this the unfortunate animal is being hunted to extinction.

ROCKET CRESS ♥♥

ROCKET CRESS (*Eruca sativa*) was grown around the phallic statues raised to Priapus the son of Venus and Bacchus the god of Wine. It was considered to be a powerful aphrodisiac – due perhaps to its being emetic (*see* Fasting). Martial, Pliny and Ovid attested to its aphrodisiac effect – the latter advising against 'lustful' rocket when disappointed in love. It was used in love potions when the woman desired her lover to increase his amatory propensity to suitable dimensions. Matthias L'Obel the herbalist tells a tale of certain monks who, roused by a cordial made of rocket, forgot their vows of continence and ran amok, ravishing all the local women. A Persian recipe 'for erection' mixes four ounces of rocket seed with one ounce of pepper and honey. As much as can be taken between two fingers is eaten night and morning.

S

SAFFRON ♥

With genial joy to warm to soul
Bright Helen mixed a mirth-inspiring bowl

ALEXANDER POPE

SAFFRON IS OBTAINED from the dried flower pistils of saffron crocus. It not only serves to make fragrant and to colour foodstuffs a rich yellow (it is under the dominion of the sun god Apollo, brother of Diana),

but it 'causes mirth and exhilaration, strengthens and restores the energies (*see* Humour). According to Bacon, the English were rendered sprightly by the liberal use of saffron. It is considered aphrodisiac in the Orient and so is frequently an ingredient of magic potions from Peking to Penzance. Cornwall is famed for its saffron cakes and buns. (The Cornish maid will occasionally add to these the hair of the *mons veneris* to awaken the ardour of a would-be-lover.)

SAMPSON ROOT (*Echinacea augustifolia*) ❤❤❤

HERBALISTS CLAIM THIS root stimulates the immune system of the body – as well as the loins. Simmer one teaspoonful in a covered cup of water for half an hour. The dose is one to six tablespoons daily.

SATYRION ❤❤❤

SATYRION IS ONE of those mysterious aphrodisiacs referred to constantly in ancient times, the exact nature of which we can only guess. Pliny said that it had but to be carried on the person to cause excitement. Petronius in his *Satyricon* mentions satyrion: 'We saw in the chambers persons of both sexes behaving in such a fashion I concluded they must every one have been drinking satyrion.' Some think it is the Satyr orchid (*Coeloglossum bracteaum*) from which the Turkish restorative drink Salep is brewed, and others credit the *Orchis mascula* (Edward Vernon in his light-hearted book on aphrodisiacs puts his money on the latter). Bagneaux de Villeneuf in *Le*

Livre d'Amour des Anciens (1927 edition) favoured the *Orchis hircina* which, when dissolved in goat's milk and given to old men, 'rekindles among them the fires of love'. Cyranus in *The Magick of Kirani King of Persia*, published in London in 1685, recommended satyrion 'for spent and barren women . . . for coition . . . it is arid and delectable and gives conception. If before coition you strew it on the virile member, anointed with honey, the women will be debilitated beyond measure. And if the women be so anointed, the intenseness of the act will be great.' Satyrion could also have been the name for an aphrodisiac cocktail or a root like vervein with a phallic shape. Such roots or those shaped like human figures, well-endowed with the appropriate male or female attributes, have always been popular for use in sympathetic love magic (remember the mandrake and Johnny the Conqueror).

SAW PALMETTO ❤❤❤

THE TERRACOTTA-COLOURED berries of the *Sarenoe serrulata* (the saw palmetto or dwarf palm) grow on the south eastern seaboard of the United States of America. They are tonic, diuretic, sedative and are said to have a stimulant effect on the breasts and the testes. I am told it is an ingredient of love potions prepared by the voodoo practitioners of New Orleans (along with other unspeakable ingredients). To prepare such a libation infuse one teaspoon of the dried berries in a cup of boiling water for ten minutes. Drink up to two cups per day iced and sweetened with honey.

SESAME SEEDS WERE used in love magic, the seed being a symbol of fertility. They are full of vitamins and minerals, especially zinc, and most restorative. An Arab powder of lavender, sesame, ginger, cloves and nutmeg promotes love.

SOUTHERNWOOD ❤❤❤

A COUSIN TO wormwood and rich in absinthol, the main ingredient of absinthe, it is a stimulating tonic and emmenagogue. Also named Lad's Love and Maiden's Ruin – need I say more!

SPANISH FLY (*Cantharides*) ♥♥♥

DESPITE ITS APPALLING record for causing suffering
and even death to those who abuse themselves by
using it, Spanish fly is probably the best known of all
aphrodisiacs and witness to the desperate measures
that man will sometimes attempt to make himself
more potent. It is obtained from the crushed *Cantharis
vesicatoria* beetle and is an irritant to the internal
organs, especially the bladder and genitals, hence its
reputation as a sexual stimulant. This itch, however,
will not subside with the act of love but persists in the
engorged parts and can drive the user to distraction.

The French have long favoured Spanish fly:
Madame de Pompadour stuffed Louis XV with it . . .
the Marquis de Sade was imprisoned for administering
Spanish fly to some unsuspecting whores with fatal

effect. Grandval in his play *Les Deux Biscuits* (1715) refers to the habit of eating confectionery containing Spanish fly:

l'un etait composé de mouches cantharides
Qui redonnent la force aux amants invalides.
(One was made of Spanish fly which gives
    strength to ailing lovers.)

In researching this book the author visited the Rue St Denis in Paris where shops selling all manner of sexual aids vie with the ladies of the night for the attention of both customer and tourist. There were only two aphrodisiacs on sale and one of these was Spanish fly. It is extremely dangerous to lace food or drink with this noxious substance, as more than the minutest amount can be lethal.

THE STRAWBERRY IS a fruit of Venus and the Virgin Mary, Queen of Heaven; since it grows so low upon the ground it is the least likely contender for the forbidden fruit!

It is used in amatory magic and found in old herbals to be recommended for anaemia. Thus it both improves and quickens the blood. A quart of strawberries a day for anaemic girls, the Victorians advised.

TANTRA

The desire which is born of nature
enhanced by art and made safe by prudence
acquires strength and security.

TANTRA IS A religion based on the sexual act which
arose in the third century A.D. in India as a reaction to
the rigours of Brahman morality. The sex act is seen
to be the gateway to eternity and the cosmic
communion that is normally achieved only after
leaving this mortal coil It is interesting to note that in
tantrism the female possesses the energy which will

bring Revelation to the male, he keeps his seed within him. On a spiritual level the man identifies with the god Shiva and the female becomes a Shakti, one of the goddesses, possessing the active energy of the God-head. 'When the serpent which is aroused within me emerges from between my two eyes they shall behold Shiva.'

TOMATOES ♥

THE TOMATO WAS introduced to Europe by the Spaniards in the sixteenth century. Named the love apple or *pomme d'amour*, its flesh is suggestive in colour and texture of the intimate parts of the body and full or iron and vitamins for vigour. The Cromwellians spread false rumour that they were poison to discourage their use, fearing their evil influence on man's morality. A delectable tomato preserve can be made by boiling tomatoes with sugar and vanilla pods.

TRUFFLES ♥♥

THIS HOMELY-LOOKING little fungus produces the same pheromone (sex smell) as does the sexually active male pig when intent on getting the female to adopt a mating position. Thus the truffle gets dispersed and does not stay put underground but is uprooted by the pig (or sometimes dog) and finds its way on to the tables of the most fortunate. The Athenians prized them as aphrodisiac and the Romans gorged on a white variety. Then they seemed to disappear until the eighteenth century at the Court of Versailles where we find Madame de Pompadour making herself quite sick on a diet of truffles, vanilla and celery in order to increase her ardour for Louis XV. Casanova, pimp to that same king, ate black truffles as aphrodisiacs. In 1936 Marcel Boulestan, gourmet writer and chef, tells that he and Colette, the great French author and lover of simple delights, once supped on 'pounds of beautiful truffles, cooked under the ashes'. This is still the best way to cook them — wash them first in wine then, having baked them, serve them hot with salt and pepper. Dai Llewellyn, known in contemporary London as the 'seducer of the valleys', swears by the truffle as the one true aphrodisiac!

TUBEROSE ♥

ONE OF THE most delicious of scents 'to seduce even the most virtuous' is that of the tuberose, the symbol of voluptuousness, a bulb with creamy white flowers that in the garden of Malay is called the Mistress of the Night so like a bride, scented and bright she comes out when the sun's away' Thomas Moore.

VANILLA ♥

VANILLA MUST BE the most delectable of all the spices. The bean from which the flavour is derived is the fermented and cured black seed pod of an orchid growing in tropical South America. Its aphrodisiac reputation is due entirely to its delicious smell and taste and to its exotic origins. The Aztecs flavoured cocoa with it and honoured Cortez with vanilla-flavoured chocolate – the Spanish introduced it to Europe in the sixteenth century. It was then lost to the world until the Marquis of Blandford reintroduced it in the nineteenth century. The Victorians thought this novelty to be most aphrodisiac. Barbara Cartland in her *Recipes for Lovers* describes a delicious ice cream made from vanilla with white grape sauce – mouth-watering!

VERVEIN ♥

CONSIDERED IN THE past to be so powerful in amatory matters that one had only to rub the hands with the juice of vervein and touch the would-be lover to win their heart. The Romans called it luck of Venus, *Veneris vena*, and believed it to be blessed with the ability to rekindle old passions. The dining-rooms of the Emperor Nero had ceilings of fretted ivory, the panels of which could slide back and let a rain of vervein and other flowers, or of perfume from hidden sprinklers, shower upon his guests to increase their merriment. The wild vervein, growing by the edge of woodlands and in sandy places, is more powerful than the cultivated one (verbena). It has pretty little flowers of a delicate mauve, with a faintly aromatic smell. Vervein contains a glucoside, verbinaline, and when taken internally flushes the liver and kidneys and deals with general debility, soothes fever and corrects painful and irregular menstruation − most venereal.

VITAMINS AND MINERALS

IT IS FASCINATING to note that the vitamins and minerals known to promote a healthy sexuality are found in great abundance in the foods long considered symbolic of fertility. So perhaps before the cynic dismisses the idea of aphrodisiacs he might consider this, for modern science has often endorsed old reputations. As Oscar Wilde said in his *Garden of Eros*, there is more in the flight of the lark than can be tested in a crucible. The body must have sufficient vitamins and minerals for health and a good love-life. It must be remembered that a deficiency or imbalance of one can affect the metabolism of another. For example, vitamin A functions together with vitamin E, and too much zinc will affect the metabolism of copper. There are certain vitamins and minerals which influence sexuality more than others (all are of course important). These are vitamin A, all the B vitamins and vitamins C and E, iron, lecithin, magnesium, phosphorus, potassium and zinc.

VITAMIN A guards against sterility and works with Vitamin E to promote normal glandular activity.

VITAMIN B1 (Thiamine) is morale boosting and controls extremes of mood, and is necessary to the conversion of food into energy.

VITAMIN B2 (Riboflavin) is necessary for healthy tissue and good eyesight. Deficiency leads to depression and exhaustion of the adrenal glands. It is found in milk, eggs, wheatgerm and dark green vegetables.

VITAMIN B3 (Niacin) is found in liver, milk, eggs and dried yeast. It helps the function of the nervous system and the circulation of blood. Without it one loses one's humour!

VITAMIN B5 (Pantothenic acid) guards against stress and depression and the greying of the hair. It is found in wholegrain cereals and liver.

VITAMIN B6 (Pyridoxine) makes for healthy skin and aids the manufacture of haemoglobin in the blood. It is found in bananas, potatoes, certain beans, wholegrain cereals and brewers yeast.

VITAMIN B12 (Cyanocobalamin) found in egg, milk and other animal products, and brewers yeast. A deficiency can lead to a weakening of the nervous system and anaemia – it is essential for the making of red blood cells.

VITAMIN B15 (Pangamic acid) oxygenates the tissues. It helps to prevent degeneration of the sexual function and senility. It is found in yeast products and apricot kernels.

VITAMIN C (Ascorbic acid) essential for the production of adrenaline and other hormones. It guards against general weakness of the system. It is found in citrus fruits and vegetables.

VITAMIN E is necessary for the production of male sex hormones which it protects from oxidation.

IRON for red blood!

LECITHIN improves the quality and quantity of sperm and must be replaced after orgasm. It is found in nuts and seeds, eggs and vegetable oils.

MAGNESIUM is important in reproduction for both sexes.

PHOSPHORUS is necessary for the maintenance of sexual desire and activity – a shortage of phosphorus will adversely affect the production of semen. Large doses will concentrate the lover's interest on erotic matters! The rich phosphorus content of fish is one of the reasons for its being held to be most aphrodisiac. Ginseng is another source.

POTASSIUM is of great value to the sexual 'athlete'. It improves the tone of the muscles and strengthens the glands of the body. Shortage of this mineral can weaken the sexual appetite and cause kidney and prostate problems. It is found in exotic fruit such as cantaloupe melons,* avocados, figs and bananas, also in vinegar.

ZINC is essential to the normal growth and health of the male sex organs. Deficiency in zinc will impair male potency — the seminal fluid and spermatozoa are rich in zinc. It is said that baldness in men is a sign of their sexual prowess, for loss of sperm means less of the zinc which is needed for healthy growth of hair (baldness and the sexual appetites can, however, both be inherited traits). The best sources are nuts and seeds, yeast, snails and oysters.

*For duty a woman, for pleasure a boy, for ecstasy a melon!

WORMWOOD (*Artemisia absinthium*) ♥♥

THIS PERENNIAL PLANT, standing up to four feet high with greenish-yellow flowers, is found world-wide. The principal agent in wormwood is absinthine, a narcotic painkiller (*see* Absinthe). To remove anxieties wormwood can be smoked or, better still, infused in a good brandy (one ounce of the flowers to a bottle of the best!) and left to stand for a month or so. If you are feeling up to it then mix the liquor with ouzo, the lifeblood of the Piraeus stevedore, and it will substitute for absinthe.

X FACTOR

THE APHRODISIAC COULD be described as the 'X factor' in sexual activity, the real but incalculable influence. The aphrodisiacs in this book are graded for effectiveness from ❤ to ❤❤ and ❤❤❤ (for the red light effect!).

YLANG YLANG

EUPHORIC AND SEDATIVE, ylang ylang relieves the tensions that are so detrimental to love. Venus is the ruling planet of this 'flower of flowers'. Ylang ylang is used in scents and amatory magic.

> If in my heart I love him
> Why should I not tell him.
> If with my body I want him
> Why should I not tell him.

FROM THE *SHIH-CHING*, CHINA, 600 BC

YOHIMBE (*Corynanthe yohimbine*)

THIS IS A large tree growing in the jungle forests of tropical West Africa. The bark of the yohimbe is aphrodisiac and used in the mating rituals of certain African tribes. The first effect experienced after taking this is one of nausea, followed by a relaxed, intoxicated state sometimes accompanied by hallucinations. It then affects the spinal nerves and increases the blood supply to the pelvic area, engorging the sexual parts. For this, one ounce of yohimbe bark should be simmered in a pint of water for twenty minutes then strained and sipped. To avoid the less pleasant effects of dizziness and nausea, 1.000 mg of ascorbic acid (vitamin C) can be added to change the alkaloids to more easily assimilated salts, yohimbine and yohimbiline ascorbate. Yohimbe may not be addictive, but if taken in excess or with alcohol or any other drugs it can be extremely dangerous.

ZODIAC

BEARING IN MIND the many other influences upon one's choice of love, here is a list of the signs of the zodiac and those with which they are thought to be most sexually compatible:

ARIES (21 March–19 April): Virgo & Scorpio
TAURUS (20 April–20 May): Libra & Sagittarius
GEMINI (21 May–21 June): Scorpio & Capricorn
CANCER (22 June–22 July): Sagittarius & Aquarius
LEO (23 July–22 August): Capricorn & Pisces
VIRGO (23 August–22 September): Aries & Aquarius
LIBRA (23 September–22 October): Taurus & Pisces
SCORPIO (23 October–21 November): Aries & Gemini
SAGITTARIUS (22 November–22 December): Taurus & Cancer
CAPRICORN (23 December–19 January): Gemini & Leo
AQUARIUS (20 January–18 February): Cancer & Virgo
PISCES (19 February–20 March): Leo & Libra

Anaphrodisiacs

'CURLERS, FACECREAMS, CHINSTRAPS and scoulies are nails in the coffin of marriage and effective antidotes to love' avows Miss Barbara Cartland. How much more so must be mouse dung ointment, snail excrement or a glow worm which Albert Magnus said 'In drink will make a Man a Eunuch'! Prudery, anxiety, ill health, over-indulgence in food or alcohol fear of intrusion, all these will unman the lover or make his lady frigid. The following pages will indicate to the lover what he must avoid to retain his libido.

ALCOHOL

MORE THAN A small quantity of alcohol impairs the sexual performance. That which in moderation can act as a stimulant by releasing inhibitions will act as a depressant on the libido if taken to excess.

ANXIETIES IN GENERAL are the death knell of things venereal. They may be inhibiting or distracting and can render the lover quite impotent. Rather than relying on drugs to alleviate this misery, try exercise or deep breathing. Robert Herrick wrote:

> To get thine ends, lay bashfulness aside;
> Who fears to ask, doth teach to be denied.

COCAINE

APPLIED TO THE the glans it may prevent premature ejaculation in the male but frequent use will wreck the nervous system and the unfortunate cocaine-user might find himself with rather less than he had bargained for.

COFFEE

THE CAFFEINE IN coffee is a nervous stimulant but not a sexual one (*see* Anxiety). There is a tale of a Persian princess who seeing several grooms attempting to restrain a stallion they were trying to geld remarked that they should save themselves the trouble and give him coffee.

AVOID SUCH FARE on sunny days when love is in the air. Venus, when Adonis died, cooled her frustrations on a bed of lettuce. And do not be misled by the apparent aphrodisiac message in the shape of the cucumber for it is really rather 'cooling'.

IMPOTENCE

HERE IS A message for the unhappy man who finds himself unable to respond to the lady fair – ninety-five per cent of cases of masculine impotence are caused by circumstances easily resolved by a little re-education – a better balanced diet with less indulgence in alcohol and nicotine, a little modest exercise, more sleep. Sometimes lack of privacy, ignorance of sexual technique, prudery or divers fears and anxieties can render the lover impotent. These problems can usually be overcome with a little thought and imagination – and a suitable partner.

NICOTINE

THE FOODS AND spices which increase the blood pressure can affect the erection to a certain extent. Nicotine acts as a depressant on the nerves, the digestion and blood pressure. Excessive smoking can undoubtedly impair the health and therefore the sexual function.

THE OPIUM POPPY, symbolic of sleep and death, was appropriately used in potions as an anaphrodisiac. Grandval, the French writer of erotic drama, refers to '*l'opium et le pavot qui font, par leurs vertus, dormir comme un sabot*' – not what the lover wants. The Chinese used it in an ointment to rub on the 'Jade stem' and 'the pearl' to prolong the act of love. The use of opium and its derivative heroin drastically diminishes the sexual powers and ultimately leads to impotence.

The clouds and rain have passed
From the heights of the Jade Mountain.
The Loving is over and slowly she dresses,
Her weak fingers fasten her robes,
Arrange her hair. And her dazed eyes
Still reflect the passionate hours.

7TH CENTURY, TUNG HAI, CHINA.

Further Reading

Gifford, Edward: *The Charms of Love*, Faber & Faber. Witty and erudite.

Hull Walton, Alan: *Aphrodisiacs from Legend to Prescription*, Associated Booksellers, Westport, Connecticut. A fascinating and informative book.

Humana, Charles & Wang Wu: *The Ying Yang: The Chinese Way of Love*, Tandem. This delightful book will introduce the reader to the unrivalled erotic literature of China.

Miller, Richard: *The Magical and Ritual Use of Aphrodisiacs*, Destiny Books. Scientific and esoteric.

Vernon, Edward: *Aphrodisiacs: An Owner's Manual*, Enigma. Tongue-in-cheek treatment of the subject.